SELF-DEFENSE FOR GIRLS is a complete course of basic self-defense for girls and women, specifically designed for use in physical education classes.

Because of the simple, practical approach to the material, this book can also be used by individuals for home study.

"... offers a simple, effective, highly intelligent approach to ... self-defense ... Highly practical in every respect, the book can be used with equal benefit by teacher, student and ordinary Jean Doe ..."

SCHOLASTIC COACH

"... Techniques are simple, easily learned ..."

JOURNAL OF HEALTH, PHYSICAL
EDUCATION AND RECREATION

"... The authors' advice is sound, and their methods could easily be demonstrated and practiced in gym classes ..."

LIBRARY JOURNAL

BOOKS BY BRUCE TEGNER

* BRUCE TEGNER'S COMPLETE BOOK OF AIKIDO AND HOLDS AND LOCKS

* BRUCE TEGNER'S COMPLETE BOOK OF JUKADO SELF-DEFENSE

* BRUCE TEGNER'S COMPLETE BOOK OF KARATE

* BRUCE TEGNER'S COMPLETE BOOK OF JUDO

* BRUCE TEGNER'S COMPLETE BOOK OF SELF-DEFENSE

  INSTANT SELF-DEFENSE (Basic)

* SELF-DEFENSE FOR GIRLS: A Secondary School and College Manual (With Alice McGrath)

* SELF-DEFENSE FOR BOYS AND MEN: A Secondary School and College Manual

  KARATE: The Open Hand and Foot Fighting

  SAVATE: French Foot and Fist Fighting

  BRUCE TEGNER METHOD OF SELF-DEFENSE

  STICK FIGHTING FOR SELF-DEFENSE

  TEACH YOUR BOY SELF-DEFENSE AND SELF-CONFIDENCE

  SELF-DEFENSE FOR WOMEN: A Simple Method (With Alice McGrath)

  KARATE, VOL. 2: Traditional Forms for Sport

  JUDO FOR FUN: Sport Techniques Made Easy

  AIKIDO SELF-DEFENSE: Holds and Locks

  JUDO AND KARATE FOR LAW OFFICERS: Defense and Control

  JUDO AND KARATE BELT DEGREES: Requirements, Rules, Regulations

  JUDO AND KARATE EXERCISES: Physical Conditioning for the Un-Armed Fighting Arts

  BLACK BELT JUDO, KARATE AND JUKADO

  KUNG FU AND TAI CHI: Chinese Karate and Classical Exercise

  SELF-DEFENSE NERVE CENTERS AND PRESSURE POINTS

* Published by Bantam Books

Other Titles in Preparation

SELF-DEFENSE
FOR GIRLS:

A Secondary School and College Manual

by
BRUCE TEGNER & ALICE McGRATH

A NATIONAL GENERAL COMPANY

SELF-DEFENSE FOR GIRLS:
A SECONDARY SCHOOL AND COLLEGE MANUAL

*A Bantam Book / published by arrangement with
Thor Publishing Company*

PRINTING HISTORY
Thor edition published December 1967
Revised, enlarged Bantam edition published November 1969

*Bantam Books are published by Bantam Books, Inc., a National
General company. Its trade-mark, consisting of the words "Bantam
Books" and the portrayal of a bantam, is registered in the United
States Patent Office and in other countries. Marca Registrada.
Bantam Books, Inc., 666 Fifth Avenue, New York, N.Y. 10019.*

PRINTED IN THE UNITED STATES OF AMERICA

ACKNOWLEDGMENTS

JAN BELLA GOLDBERG, beautiful by the evidence and bright as well, demonstrates all the defenses in this book.

LAURA D'AURI, her bright and beautiful cousin, is appreciated for her work on the manuscript.

DON PHILLIPS, mean and cranky, and his tolerant, efficient wife, HELEN, were, as usual, generous in their help.

JENINE WILLSRUD has a keen eye and a perfect sense of timing.

SGT. HANK VARAT, our favorite policeman, was kind and critical.

The authors are grateful.

CONTENTS

INTRODUCTION

Femininity and Self-Defense

Every culture has its own definition of what constitutes feminine behavior. What the culture expects strongly determines and influences that behavior. But cultural patterns and expectations change. It was not so very long ago that femininity was synonymous with helplessness. A lady was a sighing, swooning creature, totally incapable of vigorous physical activity. This concept was, of course, a highly undemocratic one as it could apply only to the privileged few! Elegant, dependent women were ladies, while their working sisters were merely females, and the exceptional active woman was dismissed as an eccentric. We no longer accept this concept of femininity. Our ideal woman is one who is poised, graceful, gentle, compassionate, and competent. No educator who expects to be taken seriously would propose that a goal of education is to foster helplessness in girls.

To teach self-defense to the ladylike girl who cherished her helplessness would have been quite impossible. For a girl who conceives of herself as feminine only to the degree that she is dependent, fainting would be the only correct and appropriate response to the threat of physical danger. However, the fact that we no longer regard helplessness as a necessary adjunct to femininity is no reason to disregard femininity as a critical consideration in teaching self-defense to girls.

Physical combat is repugnant to most girls. Fighting a man on the street is unfeminine activity in the extreme. Women can and do engage in many competitive physical activities without damage to the self-image of femininity. But consider the difference between a woman who is expert at tennis or swimming and one who gets into the ring to wrestle. Lady swimmers and tennis players are still ladies; lady wrestlers are merely freaks.

Girls and women do not have the need to ritualize aggression in "proving" fights and they do not altogether endorse the masculine inclination to do so. Girls do not need to defeat an enemy; they need only stop her intended attack. It appears that the only impulse which moves a gentle woman to violent action is not self-defense, but defense of her children.

Helplessness is the Danger

Women will run away, call for help, or try to talk their way out of a potentially dangerous situation. They will do almost anything rather than physically fight with men. It is this repugnance toward fighting which clearly contradicts the masculine concept of the degree of self-defense competence which is appropriate for girls.

There are those who claim that a little bit of self-defense instruction for girls is a dangerous thing. The proponents of that strange idea assume that if a girl has been given a small amount of self-defense instruction, she will forsake all her previous prudent actions and seek out the opportunity to show off her amazing fighting skill. Not so. Only when there is no possible alternative will a girl accept the physical encounter as a way out of a dangerous situation. Even then, self-defense is not automatic; it has to be learned. To propose that a girl who is cornered, unable to run away or get help, should know absolutely nothing, and that this is preferable to knowing a few basic techniques, simply does not make sense. Girls do not become foolish, ferocious, fighting animals because they have been prepared to meet an emergency of potential physical harm.

What is dangerous to girls who are confronted by the possibility of physical attack is not a little preparation, but no preparation at all. The panic which most girls feel when faced with an emergency, paralyzes them or leads to behavior which further endangers them. A panicky, hysterical girl may find herself unable to run away, even when it is possible. With a small amount of self-defense preparation, girls can face the threat of danger with greater poise and confidence, and thereby minimize the danger of harm. Self-defense instruction for girls should not be looked on as preparation to fight, but as preparation to face an emergency. Maggie Thomas, a senior at Sierra Joint Union High School in Tollhouse, California, expressed it excellently. Asked by a reporter why girls in that pleasant and peaceful community should need to know self-defense, Maggie replied that it was certainly as useful as life-saving and first aid.

The validity of teaching these important safety subjects does not reside in the expectation that every girl so instructed will save a life or render aid. It is the possibility that it *might* be needed which makes the instruction valid.

Movie Judo is not Self-Defense

In the movies and on television, the lady who is skilled in self-defense puts on a dazzling display of spectacular technique. No matter how large or vicious her adversary, she easily disposes of him with a showy judo throw or with a lethal karate chop to the back of the neck. In films, of course, the showy techniques succeed because the villain is a stunt man paid to fall down. Movie fight scenes are choreographed for their entertainment and shock value. Practical self-defense for real girls in actual situations is quite a different matter.

Simplicity

Our objection to difficult and complicated techniques of self-defense is not that they don't work but that they take too long to learn and cannot be remembered or used without continuing, ongoing practice. Most of the girls who are given self-defense instruction in physical education classes will not receive any additional instruction and few will engage in continuing practice. Even if the time were available for teaching advanced techniques of self-defense to girls, it would be neither practical nor desirable. Only those girls who possess special aptitude for body skills are able to learn the more complicated techniques; even they forget them without practice. All girls can learn and remember the simple techniques.

Most girls cannot readily conceive of themselves under any circumstances actually using punching, grappling, or power techniques. They reject vicious techniques. Really effective self-defense, whether for boys or girls, men or women, need not be vicious. (To propose such extreme techniques, even in self-defense, is to escalate violence.) If girls do not know simple, acceptable methods of defending themselves, they are very likely to submit to genuinely unwelcome advances rather than choose physical action which is repugnant to them. Although most girls have been told about the knee-to-the-groin defense, it is rarely used and is much less practical than is commonly supposed!

Practical, basic self-defense consists of a small "repertoire" of defense actions, easy to learn and remember. These simple actions can be combined and applied to most situations which girls might be likely to encounter. An exceptional girl, with years of instruction and practice, *might* use throwing or grappling techniques against an adversary who is heavier and taller than she is. The average girl certainly would be at an enormous disadvantage. It is likely that she would get a fast fist in the face before she could grasp her assailant for a throw, and her grappling power is far inferior to his. However, without coming into his fist range, a girl can deliver a strong blow to a vulnerable area (page 60). The total number of techniques which it is necessary to learn for basic self-defense need not exceed a dozen simple actions. In combination, they can be applied in a flexible manner to many situations.

Teacher Doesn't Need a Black Belt

Finally, we would like to propose that the most capable instructors of self-defense for girls in physical education classes are women teachers. Usually, when self-defense is taught to girls, a man is invited to teach the course. Even when they are really competent to teach girls the appropriate self-defense techniques, men teachers with extra time from their regular duties are in short supply. If teaching of self-defense is limited to the classes which are to be taught by men, the demand is not going to be met.

Because the techniques of self-defense resemble and derive from forms of Oriental fighting arts, it is a widely held opinion that only those who are very skilled in the performance of one of these arts can teach self-defense. This attitude is an impediment to acceptance of practical self-defense instruction. People who are trained in the traditional forms of the Oriental fighting arts are not prepared to teach or even to understand what is needed in the physical education class. Neither the teaching methods nor the techniques of traditional styles are suitable for the modern classroom. Moreover, proficiency ratings in judo, karate, and aikido are not given for teaching skill, but for performance skill. As you are all aware, teaching ability and performance ability are quite different crafts. Any person who has professional skill as a teacher of physical education is much better prepared to teach self-defense than a contest-oriented person without teacher training.

The aim and method of teaching girls basic self-defense is quite different from that of training men for combat. Once there is an understanding of the practical and realistic goals of self-defense instruction, it is possible to accept it as valid and useful and entirely consistent with the aims of physical education for girls.

DON'T BE A WILLING VICTIM

A Willing Victim is a Certain Victim!

It takes two to make an attack—the aggressor and the victim. It is easy enough to understand the fact that the aggressor chooses his role, but it is of great importance that you should understand that the victim has some measure of choice as well. Although the aggressor casts the parts, you may either accept or reject his choice of you as his victim. If you accept the part, then you are a *willing victim* and you ensure the success of his plan; if you reject the part, that decision *alone* may be the decisive factor in your successful defense.

You can choose another role to play in the drama of such an encounter; you can choose to manage the situation. Whether the solution is one of escape, psychological diversion or of physical defense will be determined by the particular situation. What we would like to establish firmly is that your *attitude,* your refusal to be a passive victim, is essential no matter what type of action you decide to take.

Attacks which are made on girls, whether they are serious or annoying, are made in the expectation that no defense will be offered. Because girls are not taught to defend themselves, they usually do nothing at all, or nothing effective. The feeling that they are vulnerable makes them even more vulnerable. The behavior of a passive or willing victim is easily read by the attacker. It has often been reported that a spirited show of resistance, even when the girl was not technically trained, has been enough of a defense. Because the attacker does not expect a defense, *any* defense has a chance of being successful. A girl who has a basic knowledge of self-defense can behave in such a way that she need never use the physical techniques.

There are certain important exceptions to this general rule (see When To Defend Against An Armed Adversary) but ordinarily an assailant who is faced with determination and a facade of composure will be less likely to carry out his threat of attack.

Never plead with an assailant for mercy. It doesn't work; it merely assures him of your helplessness. If you can behave as though you are angry and controlled instead of frightened, very good! An adversary is more reluctant to face up to an angered female than he is to a whiney one. Play the part, as best you can, of a fury about to be unleashed and the would-be assailant may not stick around to find out how well you can act.

WHY DON'T YOU JUST RUN AWAY?

Indeed, why not! Running away, or talking your way out of a potential physical encounter, is much more sensible and appropriate than fighting a larger, stronger, brutal adversary. And, *whenever possible,* that is exactly what you should do no matter how confident you are of your ability to defend yourself! Physical techniques for defense should be reserved for *only* those situations in which you can neither talk your way out of or run away from possible danger. If you are cornered, you have something to fall back on. If you have a reservoir of good, practical self-defense to back you in confident, poised behavior, your possibilities of talking your way out of trouble are better.

Those who advocate running away as the only solution to potential danger are not being sensible. There are situations in which it is not possible to run away. Girls do not ordinarily run as fast as men, so unless a girl has the advantage of a head start, she might not be able to outrun her adversary. In that case, turning her back on him might be the least sensible thing to do!

Because an assailant *considering* an attack on a girl may be triggered to run after her if she runs, running is only safe if there is a safe destination. Assuming that you could out-run a man, you should only run if you are certain of escape to a populated area, an occupied house, a gas station or some other refuge.

If safe refuge is not easily accessible, it is more prudent to indicate confidence, rather than fear. (See Walking Alone.)

Run when you can; make a show of confidence if you cannot. Defend with spirit if that is the only action possible!

THIS METHOD OF SELF-DEFENSE IS NEITHER JUDO NOR KARATE

... nor is it any other style of traditional un-armed fighting. Although the techniques *derive* from ancient forms of Oriental fighting, the correct, technical name for the method of self-defense which is presented in this course is—SELF-DEFENSE!

Hundreds of different names are used throughout the world to describe a small number of basic types of weaponless fighting. Whether they are called "defense" or "offense" does not change the character of the technique; it only describes the situation in which it is used.

The most common names which describe this basic group of fighting styles are boxing, judo, wrestling, karate, aikido and jiu jitsu.

That there are dozens of names by which karate is known — kung fu, kenpo, okinawa-te, etc., etc., does not change the fact that karate is the style of fighting which uses hand and foot blows. Judo is the art, mainly, of throwing. Aikido is the use of holds and locks. Jiu jitsu combines techniques from judo, karate and aikido.

None of the above, nor boxing or wrestling, is suitable as a modern method of self-defense for girls.

Because girls do not think of boxing, wrestling or karate as suitable for them, and properly so, we will briefly explain why we do not accept the traditional styles of aikido, judo and jiu jitsu as appropriate for practical, simple self-defense.

In the traditional style of training for judo-jiu jitsu, it is always assumed that unlimited training time is available to all the students; it is assumed that years of practice will follow the years of training. Because the old-fashioned teachers of judo, aikido and jiu jitsu expect every student to devote years of study, they teach complicated, difficult techniques to all students, as though every student had exceptional ability. Every student has a different degree of ability; very few are exceptional. Rather than outline a course for the exceptional student, we have selected techniques which most girls can easily learn.

Aikido, which is the form of weaponless defense using holds and locks exclusively, has been proposed as a suitable defense for women because it has the reputation of being more "gentle" than other forms, but very long training and constant practice are required before aikido can be used as a defense. It is with pride that the classical aikido teacher claims that from five to fifteen years are needed for adequate training in the use of aikido.

As a form of recreation, judo can be a splendid activity for girls, but it should not be confused with self-defense training. The aim of self-defense training is different from that of learning a pastime skill. The techniques and training procedures appropriate to sport judo are not appropriate to learning the skill of practical defense.

Jiu jitsu, in the traditional style, is not suitable for modern self-defense because it includes too many techniques, among them are those which have absolutely no application to life in our culture. Kneeling sword attack defenses are still taught in traditional jiu jitsu! Because every defense is taught against a specific attack, the student is expected to spend years learning very formal, stylized responses to hundreds of attacks.

Let us make it clear that years of training in *any* style of defense would give adequate preparation in self-defense training. We are not assuming years of training, but *hours* of training; thus, the need to select only those techniques which meet the needs of girls taking a short course in basic self-defense.

This course presents a small number of techniques which are effective in most of the situations you might ever encounter. Ten years from now it will be easier to remember how to use a dozen techniques than it would be to remember hundreds.

Learning self-defense is no more difficult than learning to drive a car. You learn to drive a car with a few hours of instruction, but it takes considerably more training and practice to become a race driver. You learn to swim in a few hours, but it takes years of training and practice to become a champion swimmer.

Because you are not training to become an expert, you can learn in a very short time what used to be thought to take *years* of training. You are not being trained for contest judo or for mastery of aikido. You will not be required to fight a Samurai warrior in your final exam. Although the techniques are based on the ancient Oriental arts of weaponless fighting, what you are learning is simply — SELF-DEFENSE!

WHAT DOES BASIC MEAN?

Most attacks and frightening situations which are encountered by girls and women are not the extreme ones we read about in the paper. Statistically, those attacks are not common; it is precisely for this reason that we read about them. The most common attacks are variations of the situations which are shown in this course. Most girls should be able to use the material taught here in most situations which they are likely to encounter.

Most girls and women go through their entire lives without being threatened by what we could call an "attack." By teaching you some basic methods of dealing with the possibility of attack, the nervous fear of helplessness which is felt by most girls, can be removed. Fear leads to panic; removal of the fear can help avoid many situations in which the fear and panic are exactly the factors which endanger a girl. The composure which comes of feeling that you are not altogether helpless, can help you to behave in such a manner that you do not betray fear and do not encourage a threatened attack.

A little learning is a *very* good thing in this instance. It does not invalidate the usefulness of the advice nor of the defense methods to acknowledge that there are some situations for which no amount of training can prepare you. Also, there are some situations in which a defense could be made only by a person who had been very highly trained.

Rather than waste your energy and fray your nerves with useless worry about what you cannot do, you *can* learn to take care of yourself in the best possible manner for the greatest number of situations. In a minimum amount of time, without much practice, and assuming that you have no special aptitude, you can learn a handful of useful defensive actions which will give you adequate protection for most of the situations with which you might be confronted.

THE PERIL OF PANIC—Guns Are Not The Answer!

In spite of lurid newspaper and magazine horror stories, you are not in constant danger of attack upon your life and honor. To live as though you were, would be to live in a state of hysteria.

We have heard it seriously proposed that every home ought to have a "security" room—a room with extra heavy doors, bars on the windows, independent power source, a phone and . . . a gun!

Aside from the fact that it is a cynical and dangerous proposal, it is impractical for girls, especially. Most girls are as frightened of guns as they are of being attacked. *ORDINARY* precaution is enough to minimize the greatest part of danger of attack. It would be almost impossible to predict and prepare for the extra-ordinary, even if we were to convert every home into a fortress or arsenal. Surely we all feel more safe in a community where sensible and cautious behavior is used as a preventive than in one where every home has a loaded gun!

The further arguments against guns for defense for girls are based on legal, moral and emotional grounds. A gun can be used, and guns often are used, in a state of panic. Once the panic has passed, the responsibility for the shooting remains. It is a great emotional shock to kill someone; it is a great emo-tional shock to stand trial for murder.

In the U.S. there are so very, very few instances of justified gun killings compared with the accidental and homicidal use of guns that to urge the placing of great numbers of weapons in the hands of those least emotionally able to handle them seems a most irresponsible proposal.

SPORTSMANSHIP—IS IT PART OF SELF-DEFENSE?

Girls, generally speaking, do not suffer from the same disadvan-tage as do boys in American culture; boys are expected to be "good sports" no matter what happens to them, but girls, it is recognized, are not under such an unfair obligation. For it is unfair, whether we are talking about boys or girls, to handicap them with the restrictions of sportsmanlike behavior *when the opponent is not performing under the same set of rules.*

A sport is a game in which both partners or opponents are participating voluntarily. In a sport, the conditions of participa-tion are set by rules and both participants are expected to abide by those conditions. In a sport, the participants are usually matched as closely as possible according to skill or size, or both. With the exception of boxing, we can think of no sport in which the goal is to hurt your opponent.

On the street, you are not playing for points; you are faced with an adversary who will use any means to harm, injure or frighten you. Is it good sportsmanship to choose to fight someone small-er than you, someone you assume is incapable of making an adequate defense, someone who would decline to fight if given the sportsmanlike option of making the choice? Is it good sport for several people to attack one victim? Is it a sport to fight without any rules? Well, obviously the answer must be no. In view of that, does it not seem unfair to ask girls (or boys) to limit their defenses to "sportsmanlike" techniques. Keep sportsmanship in games where it belongs.

IS ANYTHING MISSING?

Two of the common misconceptions about self-defense are: 1. The notion that you have to learn judo falls, and be thrown, in order to learn self-defense. 2. That a kick into the groin is the most important thing a girl can learn for self-defense. Neither is true.

Safety falls are useful to know, but they are not necessary for self-defense. Learning judo falls and learning to throw and be thrown is sport judo. In sport judo the throws are the essential techniques; that's what sport judo is about. In practical, basic self-defense, throwing is not essential. In this course, therefore, you do not need to learn the judo falls.

It is a trite concept that the best thing a girl can do is kick into the groin for self-protection. A kick into the groin is indeed very painful and very effective when it is applied. It is not possible to deliver a groin kick without coming in very close to your adversary and putting yourself into his fist range. Unless you are already that close in, it does not make good sense to put yourself within fist striking range. Men can usually deliver a fist blow faster than you could move in to deliver a knee kick. Men have an instinctive reaction to protect the groin area. And girls, it is interesting to note, have a natural reluctance to kicking into the groin, even in justified self-defense. For all these reasons, the kick into the groin is not a technique which we favor. Other simple, effective techniques will do as well.

Aside from these examples of deliberate omission, there are hundreds of techniques, perhaps, thousands, which do not appear in this text. We have selected only those which we feel are consistent with the aims of the course and which are suitable for the level of skill which is aimed at.

RULES OF SELF-PROTECTION AT HOME

Many victims of assault in the home have been unwitting accomplices to the crime; they have failed to obey the simple, basic rules of self-protection.

If you follow these rules, you will minimize the possibility of frightening or dangerous situations. These are good rules for every home; they are especially important if you are home alone.

DO NOT ALLOW ANYONE TO ENTER YOUR HOME UNLESS YOU KNOW HIM.

KEEP DOORS AND WINDOWS LOCKED: KEEP WINDOWS COVERED AT NIGHT.

KEEP A SAFETY CHAIN ON THE FRONT AND BACK DOORS; USE THEM.

HAVE A VIEWER OR SIGHTHOLE INSTALLED IN YOUR DOOR.

DO NOT MAKE PUBLIC THE KNOWLEDGE OF TIMES WHEN YOU ARE HOME ALONE AT NIGHT, OR IF YOU ARE HOME ALONE REGULARLY.

INSTALL EFFECTIVE LOCKS.

Don't Invite Trouble

If you leave your doors and windows open or unlocked, or if you open your door at the request of a stranger, you could be inviting trouble.

The most common method of gaining entry is to pose as a legitimate caller—a messenger, repairman, salesman, or poll-taker, for instance. Do not allow a stranger to enter unless you have personally made arrangements for the call. If you do not expect the man who says he has come to service an appliance or to test equipment, first talk to him through the viewer or with the safety chain on.

Before you allow a stranger entry, be certain he has legitimate business. Check with his office by phone. If you cannot confirm his legitimate reason for being in your house, DO NOT LET HIM IN! Anyone with a legitimate reason for calling will not insist on entering if you refuse him. It is better to refuse entry to a legitimate caller than it is to invite possible danger into your home.

Insure Safety With Proper Locks

Not all locks are effective. Some can be opened easily. Maximum safety can be insured by getting a licensed, bonded locksmith to check your door and window locks.

At least, consult with a reliable hardware store about the relative safety of the various kinds of locks. It is probably true that the better locks will be more expensive. The cheapest insurance you can buy is the installation of adequate locks.

A bad habit (and a common mistake) is to keep the front door locked and leave the back door unlocked.

Install safety chains on all doors which lead outside. Get into the habit of using them. It is the *habit* of using the safety chain at all times which is your protection.

Install a viewer or sighthole in your door so that you can see who is there without opening the door at all. Get into the habit of using the viewer.

Hidden Keys

Everybody knows the "secret" hiding places for keys. The first place an intruder looks for a key is under your mat, over the door jamb, and in the nearest flower pot. If you must leave keys around the house, use some imagination to hide them.

Lights Deter Prowlers

Prowlers prefer the dark. Inside and outside lights give you a good deal of protection. Leave lights on at night, even when you are away from home. Change the location of the lights from room to room.

Outside lights should be placed where they illuminate your doors, particularly.

Automatic switches are not expensive and can be used to turn lights off and on if you are away.

Keep it Quiet

Don't broadcast the fact that you are home alone, particularly if you are alone much of the time.

A woman living alone should not put her first name on the mailbox and should list her initial, not her name, in the phone book.

HOW TO USE THE TELEPHONE TO GET HELP

The telephone is your best friend if you are prepared to use it properly.

To get help from the operator, you do not have to know the phone number of the emergency call you want to make. The telephone operator is trained to help you in an emergency; you only need to give her the information in as calm a voice as you can manage: she needs the phone number you are calling from first; then give the address and your name and then describe very briefly what kind of emergency help is needed. If she asks you to stay on the line, do so; if she asks you to hang up, follow her instructions.

If you practice mentally the procedure for getting help on the phone, you will be ready to use it.

ALWAYS when walking or driving alone, carry change for making a telephone call.

TELEPHONE "DON'TS"

DO NOT give out your phone number indiscriminately; especially if you live alone or are home alone regularly.

DO NOT volunteer information about yourself to strangers on the phone. Especially, do not volunteer the information that you are home alone.

Babysitting is a special situation in which you should mentally practice the kind of reply you make to people who phone. For instance, instead of saying "Mr. and Mrs. Timberlake have gone out for the evening and I am the babysitter" you can say "Mr. Timberlake is not here now, may we take a message." The first way of phrasing the information implies a young girl alone; the second way of phrasing the reply is ambiguous. If you think about this situation before it happens, you will be ready with an appropriate response.

THE UNFRIENDLY PHONE

Obscene and nuisance callers rarely offer any threat of physical danger but, unless handled properly, they may persist in their calls for the perverse pleasure they get out of alarming and upsetting their "victims."

If the phone rings and there is silence when you answer it, or an obscene remark is made, hang up immediately. If you can, report the call to the operator right away. Sometimes the caller will not leave the line and you might have to use a different telephone to report him. Whether or not you have reached the operator, if the nuisance caller phones again, you can tap the cradle button and say "Operator, this is the call I want traced."

Persistent offensive calls *must* be reported to the phone company and you should follow their instructions for getting rid of the nuisance, even if it means accepting a change of phone number.

WALKING ALONE

If you can possibly avoid it, don't walk alone at night on dark streets. If you cannot avoid it, take a few precautions which will help to protect you.

Walk toward the curb side of the sidewalk, well away from buildings. This minimizes the possibility of being grabbed from a doorway or building entrance.

Carry a whistle. If you think you are in danger, use it.

Have change for making a telephone call whenever you are alone.

If you walk alone at night, carry a small flashlight. Flashing a light as you enter a parking lot, before you get into your car, and as you approach an area which might conceal danger, will minimize the possibility of attack. The mere fact of flashing a light indicates an awareness and preparation which help to protect you.

IS SOMEONE FOLLOWING YOU?

If you think you are being followed, turn to look at the possible source of danger. This is very, very important.

If you keep your back turned because you are too frightened to look, you are only placing yourself in more danger. If you turn around to face the situation, you can evaluate whether or not there is a threat.

It is not always possible to tell the difference between a potential threat or another person like yourself merely walking down the same street, but in most cases you could make the decision based on what you see. What you imagine can sometimes be more terrifying than reality.

If you are worried by what you see, you can be prepared to avoid the danger or defend yourself. If you think you can outrun the threat and there is a safe refuge, you can run. If you cannot run, you could cross the street and walk resolutely in the opposite direction. This is one way of signalling that you are aware of the threat, but you are not in a panic. You could put your hand in your purse to get a purse weapon (see Purse Weapons); this action also signals determination, rather than helplessness. It is normal to feel fear in threatening situations, but you should try to avoid showing your fright. Police reports verify the fact that a man who is considering an attack on a girl or woman may decide against the attack because of her show of willingness to defend herself in some way.

If there is no possibility left but physical defense actions, you are more protected if you face an adversary than if you leave yourself vulnerable to attack from the rear.

Repeat: If you think you are being followed, turn to see what is happening.

GETTING INTO ELEVATORS

If you cannot avoid using an elevator alone at night, take some precautions:

Have a whistle in your hand, ready to use. Otherwise, be prepared to scream if necessary. If there is a strange man waiting to get on the same elevator, let him go on without you and wait for the elevator to return. But do not show by your behavior that you are afraid. A calm exterior (no matter what you feel inside), is protection.

Make mental preparation to defend, if necessary. Don't be caught by surprise.

SCREAMING

Screaming is one of the best deterrents to attack. Many intended attacks have been foiled with loud screams. You should use screaming as an aid to any of the other defense actions you have learned. Yelling, especially sudden, unexpected yelling, is disconcerting and distracting and is very useful to your defense. The exceptions to be noted are two. First, if you are being robbed and not threatened with physical harm you should be quiet. Second, if your assailant is known to be or seems to be insane, your best defense is physical action; screaming may only infuriate a deranged person further. But, qualified by these two exceptions, train yourself to SCREAM for your life.

DRIVING ALONE SAFELY

The first rule of safety if you drive alone is SAFETY CHECK YOUR CAR. The less chance there is of auto trouble, the less chance of being stranded in a strange place.

When you are driving alone in a place and time in which there is possible danger, follow these rules to minimize possibility of attack:

Keep all windows rolled up and safety buttons down. If you need to keep any window open, keep the driver's side open and be prepared to roll it up at any sign of danger.

It is especially important to remember to keep the door and window of the passenger side of the car secured; this is the side most vulnerable to entry.

Under no circumstances allow a stranger to enter your car. If you are driving alone and someone signals you that there is something wrong with your car, do *not* open your car to him, instead, drive immediately to the nearest service station or to some area where there are other people and check it out then. Better to risk damage to your car than risk damage to yourself.

Remember your horn; it can bring help if you need it.

If you can avoid parking in dark, uninhabited areas, do so, even if it means a parking fee; it could be very inexpensive insurance.

Even in the daytime when a girl gives or accepts a ride from a stranger, it is a risk.

Carry change for a telephone call if you are driving alone

If you are driving alone and see someone on the road who is apparently having car trouble, DO NOT STOP. You can be a good citizen and help the stranded driver without risk to yourself. Note the location of the stranded car; note the color and type of car and the make. Drive on to the nearest gas station, police station or telephone and report the trouble. You need not know the phone number to make a report. Tell the telephone operator about the emergency and she will connect you with the appropriate agency or person.

COMMERCIAL "PROTECTIVE" WEAPON DEVICES

We do not recommend any of the commercial devices which are widely advertised as defense weapons for girls and women.

Many of these devices have been reported as being unreliable and ineffective. Dependence upon such devices makes you more vulnerable if the so-called protective device is out of reach or does not function.

In some states, the devices are illegal.

DOGS FOR DEFENSE?

If you own a dog, it is a good idea to take it with you if you are driving or walking at night. A dog, even a little one, will act as a deterrent. At home, a barking dog will usually discourage entry. However, you must not depend on a dog to protect or defend you unless it has been trained to do so.

If you do not enjoy having a dog around, you will have to weigh the possible protection you would get against the nuisance of ownership — a completely subjective decision.

REPORTING AN ENCOUNTER—YOUR SOCIAL DUTY

It is very seldom that a criminal attack is made by a person only once in his life. The pattern of such behavior is repetitious.

If you have had an unpleasant encounter, whether or not you have been hurt, your most responsible action is to report the incident to the police—as soon as possible. By doing so, you may prevent harm or injury to other girls.

If obscene or offensive behavior is directed at you, physical or verbal, the police should be given as much information as you can provide. The more information the police have, the more possible it is for them to apprehend the offender. In mental practice, prepare yourself to note the following: Height, age, weight and build, color of eyes and hair, type and color of clothes, type of voice; if armed, was the weapon held in the right or left hand. If a car is involved, note make, style, color.

ONGOING DEFENSE

In most cases of attempted attack, the very first action which is applied is enough to stop the attack. As most attacks on women and girls are made by men who expect *no resistance whatsoever,* the resolute and determined manner in which you apply the first action and the fact that you have hurt him, is enough to disconcert, confuse and discourage him. A *display* of courage has been enough to stop a good many intended attacks—but these stories do not make the headlines.

If the first action does not stop the attack, then you must continue. The idea of ongoing, continuing action is essential. Even when you are using a single technique, such as the kick into the knee or shin, it becomes an ongoing, continuing defense if you do it over and over until your adversary is subdued or sufficiently hurt to permit you to run away.

COMPLETE DEFENSES

Although a single technique used over and over could be a complete defense, in the sense that it will be effective for release or escape, a combination of the simple actions is more efficient and this combination is what we refer to as being complete defense.

In the beginning of the course, you will do each technique separately because this is the learning procedure. In the examples of the use of each technique we show you when that particular technique might be the essential action, the one most important to your defense. But, the combination of the techniques in a flexible manner is the vital concept of the course.

MENTAL PRACTICE

You have been told that the defenses in this book do not require years-long training and they do not require practice to make them available to you ten years from now, or whenever you might need them. What will keep them fresh in your mind is mental practice.

It has recently been established that skills can be retained almost as well through mental practice as they can through practice of the actual techniques. After having learned a procedure, the person who *thinks it out,* who goes over it in his mind, loses very little of his ability to perform the procedure compared with those who engage in performance practice. This means that you can keep your training fresh and usable by giving it some thought. You can improve the practical value of your training by thinking about applications to possible situations.

Mental practice involves effort and concentration, but not a great deal of time. Set problems for yourself in which you are faced with a situation in which you use your training. You do it with a perfect mixture of calm control and spirited action. It is like directed day-dreaming with a defined focus. You need not spend great, long periods brooding about the potential danger of attack in order to accomplish this. An occasional review, a thinking out of the possible situation and your response to it could save your life. Less dramatic and more likely, it could save you embarrassment and pain.

SAFETY IN PRACTICE

Many years of research and teaching experience have gone into the selection of the material which is presented in this course. There is ample evidence that these techniques will work. In class, you are not trying to *prove* that they work; you are simply going to learn them.

In order to learn, you need not inflict great pain on your training partner; you need not endure more than the slightest pain (to the point which indicates that the technique is being applied properly.) It is neither necessary nor desirable to be rough or to tolerate rough, careless work.

Obey the rules of safety to the letter.

TAPPING FOR SAFETY

The signal for stopping your partner is tapping. Tapping is a better signal than talking, because your voice may not always be audible in a room full of girls practicing. The best signal is to tap your partner, because that gets the fastest response, but you can tap yourself or the floor if that is more convenient. Tap when you feel pain; tap when a technique is applied correctly; tap if your partner is working in a rough manner.

IMMEDIATELY upon feeling or hearing the tapping signal from your partner, you must stop. If you work with a partner who ignores the tapping signal or who consistently works in a rough manner, you should ask for a different partner. It is not brave, it is foolish to continue working with a partner who ignores the safety rules. When safety rules are followed, there is no reason why anyone should be hurt in this course.

SURPRISE IS YOUR WEAPON, TOO—And Why These Techniques Will Not Work Against Friends

Most girls are so delighted with the techniques of self-defense which they learn in the first lesson, that they can hardly wait to leave class to try them out. Take heed: these techniques do not work against friends; they only work when you mean them to! Playing around with defense techniques is very ineffective because you don't really mean to hurt your friends. For example, a forceful kick into the shin is extremely painful; but you would not want to demonstrate how very painful it is if you were trying it out with a friend. In class, your partner is working with you to help you learn; outside of class, your friendly opponent is not acting as your learning partner. It is very disappointing to try out your new skill only to discover that it doesn't seem to work. It works when you are serious about it!

As we have repeated (because it is important), an actual assailant does not expect any effective defense; any opponent, even a friendly one, becomes a more difficult adversary if you put him on his guard. You would never think of warning your opponent in a game that you were going to try a particular shot or play, so why give away your advantage in this activity where surprise could be the success factor.

DISTRACTION

If you can distract your adversary for an instant, it will aid your defense.

Against an adversary who is threatening to attack or who is moving in slowly, a distraction can be used to direct his attention to the diverting movement or sound.

If there is anything to throw, throw it. It does not necessarily have to be an object which will hurt him and your aim does not have to be perfect. A handkerchief, lipstick, book, ashtray, anything which can be thrown will serve the purpose—to divert. The natural reaction to a thrown object is to duck. As he ducks, you begin your defense.

If your assailant is standing still, threatening you, your distraction can be subtle—an eye movement, a whispering, a slight head movement. The natural reaction to such gestures or sounds will give you a fraction of a moment of precious time in which to make your next move.

A loud, unexpected yell can be the most effective diversion. For the important exceptions, see SCREAMING.

Even in the case of a rushing attack, a loud yell as you begin your defense action could serve as a distracting element.

Use distraction as a preliminary to defense actions whenever possible.

HOW TO FOLLOW INSTRUCTIONS

If you are getting instruction in a physical education class, recreation center or Y, your teacher will provide the method of study.

If you are using this text for a home study course, here are some guidelines which may help you get the most out of your practice. The advice which follows is based on the assumption that you will be practicing without the supervision or help of a professional teacher. The advice would apply to a team of two or to a group.

Partners

Although the instruction is illustrated throughout by a girl (librarian Jan Goldberg) working with a man (co-author Bruce Tegner), it is common for two girls to work together to learn self-defense. In many cases it is more successful for two girls to learn together than for a girl to work with a man, especially if the man is not fully cooperative. Resisting the technique is not a good learning procedure; cooperation is more useful. Men frequently need to prove that they are physically superior to women; they tend to resent the role of the vanquished villain. Girls working together have no need to "prove" anything to each other. They can concentrate on learning.

Working with a fully cooperative male partner is, of course, a perfectly acceptable way of learning.

Whether your partner is a man or a woman, in beginning practice offer no resistance to the technique. When partners have learned the correct manner of applying the technique, then you can offer slight resistance. As partners become better acquainted with the defense actions, the resistance can be increased. Just remember that you cannot, in training, really hurt your partner as though he or she were a serious adversary.

Without professional supervision, you must be particularly certain that you read and follow the safety rules: No rough work. Tapping for safety. Work for understanding of the techniques, rather than for speed.

How to Practice

First, read the text completely through. This will give you an understanding of the goals of the course and will acquaint you with the attitudes upon which the instruction is based. Then, scan the photos. Examine them to become familiar with the gestures and physical relationships.

Then, after you have thus become quite familiar with the book, begin to practice the techniques. Although physical education teachers may, and do successfully, change the order of presentation of the material, students learning this as a home study course will do best by following the instruction from beginning to end, in the order shown.

The suggested time interval for each period of home study is one-half hour. The lessons should be as frequent as is allowed by your personal schedule; daily if possible, or three times a week if that is practical, once a week if no closer intervals can be arranged.

If you complete the instruction and are interested in reaching a higher level of skill, repeat all the material with greater emphasis on technical perfection. Partners will find that they can more easily see and correct errors on each other than on themselves. Frequent reference to the photos will help you detect and correct mistakes. Read the text more than once to be certain that you have the right idea about the technique.

The highest level of proficiency is reached when you have learned all the basic material and can make combinations smoothly, utilizing the full range of known material and alternating right and left hand and foot blows.

CORRECTING MISTAKES

If you were trying to become an expert in the fighting arts, it would be necessary to reach a high level of technical skill. For basic self-defense this is not necessary.

All new students make mistakes. In the text you will be reminded of essential points and cautioned to watch out for the most common errors. These corrections have been kept to a minimum, consistent with the aims of the course.

To accelerate your training, observe these reminders from the very first day of practice.

1   2

STRONG AND WEAK BALANCE

If you assume a position of strong balance which we call the T-position, you can avoid falling down if you are pushed or shoved.

1.   From a natural, standing position you are very vulnerable to even a small amount of pushing force. With fingertip pressure you can be placed in a very weak, off-balance position; you have no resistance. (You will take advantage of this weakness when you apply some of the defenses.)

2.   If you place one foot forward and place the other foot at right angles to it, forming a T-position, you are in a much stronger stance. From this position you can resist quite a heavy pushing force without falling backward. Get into the habit of standing in a T-position, when appropriate, during the practice of the defenses.

USING YOUR OPPONENT'S STRENGTH

Strength is not the critical factor in successful application of self-defense techniques. You will, of course, be expected to use the considerable strength at your disposal (we all have much more power than we ever use or are conscious of), but you will not try to match your strength against that of a larger, heavier adversary.

3. No matter how much you push, you cannot hope to oppose the resistance of someone larger and more powerful than you are.

3

4

5

4, 5. But, if instead of opposing his strength, you *use* it, you can make him contribute to his own defeat. Here we show what happens when you step quickly to the side as he pushes, pulling him into the direction in which he is forcing himself and twisting him into awkward, off-balance position.

The foregoing are two examples of body mechanics which are applied in self-defense techniques. You need not learn all the principles upon which the techniques are based, but you should understand that there are factors other than strength and power which you can use to your advantage.

OPEN HAND BLOW: Striking With The Edge
Of The Hand

Girls find it difficult and awkward to hit with the fist in characteristic male style. An open hand method of striking, using the outside edge of the hand is more practical and more versatile.

The fleshy part of the hand is the area to be used for striking; avoid hitting with the little finger or wrist bones and keep the hand slightly cupped. The thumb is held against the forefinger; fingers are held firm, but not rigid.

You can test the correctness of the striking position by hitting lightly onto a table or any hard surface. When the proper hand position is used, there is no pain felt even when you hit with great force. With the edge of the hand, you can hit with either hand with almost equal effectiveness.

The target areas you should aim for are:

6.   Onto the forearm muscle.

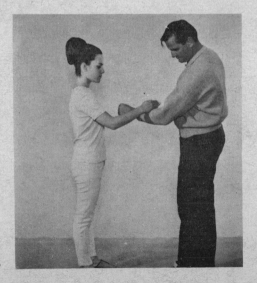

6

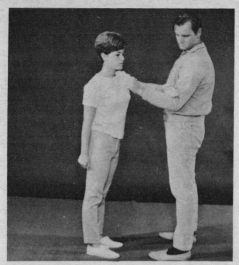

7

7. Into the bend of the elbow.

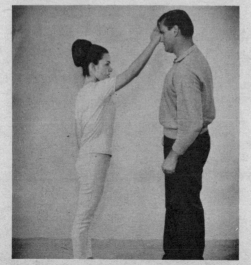

8

8. Onto the nose, or up under the nose.

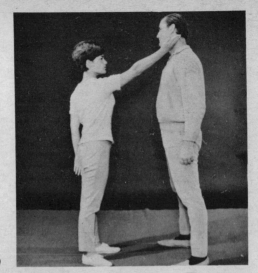

9

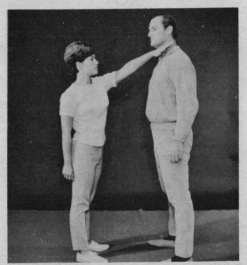

10

9, 10.   Into the side of the neck, using either hand.

Striking with force onto the forearm muscle can result in numbing the arm and even a moderate blow causes pain because of nerves centered in this area.

Striking into the crook of the elbow bends the arm and causes pain.

Striking onto the nose causes a great deal of pain, but, contrary to the popular notion, it is not a dangerous blow. (Boxers hit each other on the nose with enough force to break it, but do not suffer serious injury as a result.)

Striking into the side of the neck is effective, without being dangerous. At the side of the neck are nerves, veins and arteries, exposed and vulnerable. A moderate blow will cause pain; but more important than the pain is the stunning effect and the disorientation which results. A heavy blow, one which a girl could deliver by releasing all her available strength, could render a man unconscious.

The edge-of-the-hand blow can be used with one or both hands, cross-body or back-handed and from many different positions. The target areas should be memorized; they are the places to strike for greatest effectiveness.

Avoid holding your hand rigid and flattened; a slight cupping is more efficient.

11. Remember to keep your thumb against your index finger; *not* extended, as shown in the photo.

Avoid hitting with your wrist bone or finger bone.

Correct this common error.

11

EXAMPLES OF USE OF THE OPEN HAND BLOW

Here are some examples of the many applications of the edge-of-the-hand blow.

12, 13.   Assailant reaches out as though to grab; slash with edge of the hand onto the forearm muscle or into bend of the elbow; follow with double-handed slash into both sides of his neck.

12

13

14

15

14, 15. Assailant has gripped the wrist; a slash into the bend of the elbow, followed by a slash into the side of the neck.

16. Assailant has made a front body grab; double-handed slash into both sides of the neck.

Whenever the assailant is close in, and one or both your hands are free, you can apply the edge-of-the-hand slashing defense.

16

FINGER STAB

Stabbing with the fingers is useful for close-in attacks and may be used in one manner against vicious attacks and in a modified fashion against less violent attacks.

With the fingers held close together, very slightly cupped and rigid, use a quick stabbing motion.

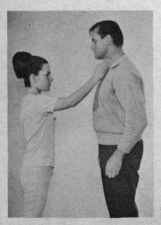

17. With the palm held vertical, stab into the neck muscle, to the side of the windpipe.

17

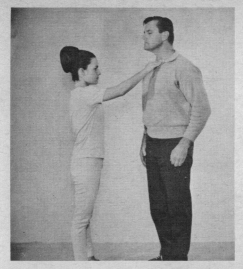

18

18. With the palm down, stab into the hollow of the throat.

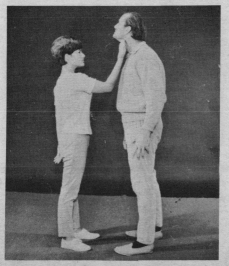

19

19. With the palm up, stab upward under the jaw.

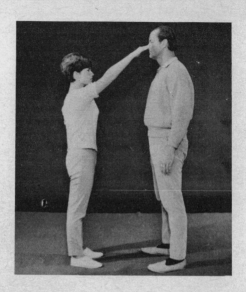

20

20. Stab into the eyes.

By stabbing with your fingertips into the neck at the side of the windpipe, 17, or upward under the jaw, 19, it is possible to inflict pain to show that you are seriously trying to defend yourself, without injuring your adversary. Because many of the situations in which young girls are defending themselves will involve an adversary who is not vicious, but overly persistent, it is important to distinguish between defenses in such cases and defenses against a really vicious assailant.

Stabbing into the eyes is justified in the event of vicious attack. Against an assailant who intends great harm, the eye stab is an effective and appropriate defense.

Stabbing into the hollow of the throat, 18, (the windpipe), is a serious blow which could result in injury and might even be fatal. Its use is justified against a vicious attack.

Remember to keep your hand slightly cupped for finger stabs.

EXAMPLES OF USE OF FINGER STABS

21.   Man is making an attempt to grab or hug but he is **not** attempting harm or injury; stab into the neck.

22.   Man is not discouraged by blow into the side of the throat, or he has made clear a more serious intent; stab into throat hollow.

21

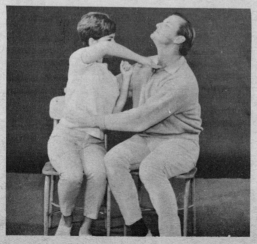

22

23

23. Man clearly intends serious harm (whether choking or similar close-in situation); stab into eyes.

HEEL-OF-THE-PALM BLOW

This easy action can be applied by any girl or woman. It is effective against a much stronger, larger person and it can be used seated or standing. Applied with force, when it is not expected, it can cause a man to fall to the ground.

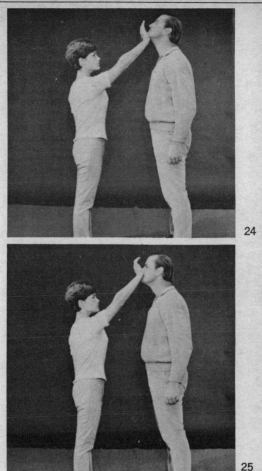

24

25

24, 25. Cupping the hand, strike up under the chin or under the nose.

A variation of this blow is hitting with the Y of the hand, the area between the thumb and forefinger. It can be used up under the nose.

In practice of the heel-of-the-palm blow, avoid simulating a pushing action; the proper delivery is a snappy thrust. Pushing is the proper delivery for the Y-of-the-hand blow.

EXAMPLES OF USE OF HEEL-OF-PALM BLOW

26, 27, 28.   The action is most useful in situations similar to those pictured here, where the man is already grabbing or hugging.

26

27

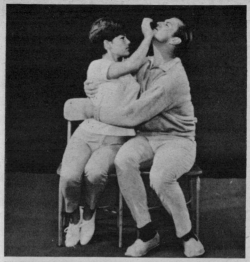

28

29

29.   The Y of the hand is used up under the nose.

Whenever possible, do not step in close to an adversary to apply a defense; if you are out of his reach, stay there. Close-in defenses are for use only when you cannot avoid being close to your adversary.

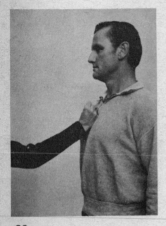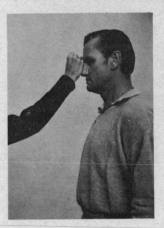

30   31

SIDE-OF-FIST BLOW

The two most common mistakes which are made by girls who
try to defend themselves against a stronger assailant are: a.
Trying to squirm or struggle out of a body grab; b. Beating tiny
little fists against a man's chest, as in 30. The chest is a useless
target.

31.   The very same blow when aimed at a vulnerable target is
effective. Striking onto the nose causes pain and disorientation.

When practicing the side-of-the-fist blow, remember to keep
your thumb placed outside of your fingers. Avoid hitting with
your little finger; it is the muscle area of the fist which is the
striking point.

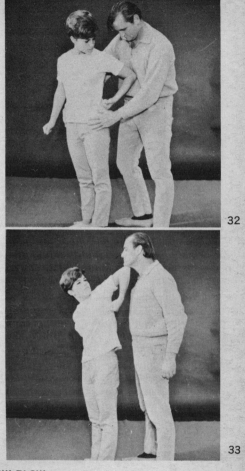

32

33

ELBOW BLOW

Hitting with the elbow is useful against an adversary attacking from the rear. The elbow is used for striking into the mid-section, 32, or into the face, 33.

You *must* turn to look at your target when you practice the elbow blow to the rear. It is more efficient to deliver an elbow blow with your palm up, as shown.

EXAMPLES OF USE OF ELBOW BLOW

34. Adversary starts to grab, or has grabbed loosely; whenever the body space permits, strike back forcefully into the midsection.

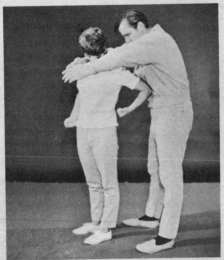

34

35

35.   If he has already grabbed and is holding you close, turn to look at what you are doing, and hit up into the face. As he pulls his head away from the blow, turn your head and strike an elbow blow from the opposite direction with the other arm.

36   37

KNUCKLE JAB

The use of this technique is limited to situations in which the adversary is merely annoying. You can cause enough discomfort to convince him that you will not tolerate his bullying, but it is not an adequate defense for more serious situations.

36, 37.   Against a grab as shown, or in a similar situation, dig into the side of the body with the middle knuckle of your fist extended. The target point is about two inches up from the waist. A digging, grinding action causes pain.

In practice of the knuckle jab, keep your thumb outside your fist. As shown in 37, your palm must be turned up for efficient use of the technique.

38

THUMB PRESS INTO THROAT

This technique is limited to those situations in which the adversary is very close, very determined to get closer, but is not trying to hit or injure you.

38. As he grabs, place your thumb into the hollow of the throat just below the windpipe. (Do not jab or stab into this area unless the attack is vicious.) A gentle, pressing action will be sufficient; if he tries to move forward, he hurts himself.

This technique is easy to do from a seated position, as well as standing. Use the tip of your thumb, not the flat area.

FINGER PULLING

This very easy action has many uses. Its virtue lies in the fact that even a big man with a strong grip cannot resist the action of your hand against one of his fingers.

The action is merely to grip one of his fingers (try to grip the small finger, it is the weakest), and pull it away with a jerky motion. The action will make him release the grip, or will weaken it considerably.

See the section COMPLETE DEFENSES for an explanation of "what to do next." As is true of all the simple techniques taught in this book, finger pulling is to be thought of as an action which can be combined with other actions to make complete defenses.

When practicing the finger pulling defenses, avoid grasping with the tips of your fingers; try to get a good firm grip with your hand. Instead of trying to twist the captured finger away from you, use a jerky vigorous action to effect release.

EXAMPLES OF USE OF FINGER PULLING

39, 40.   In this situation, the man is not trying to harm or hurt you, but is making unwelcome advances; take his wrist as though in a friendly fashion and then pull back on his little finger.

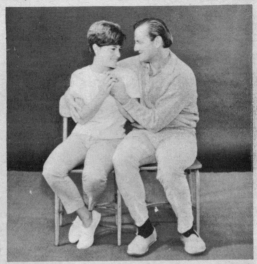

39

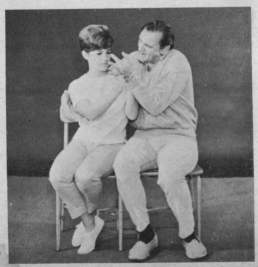

40

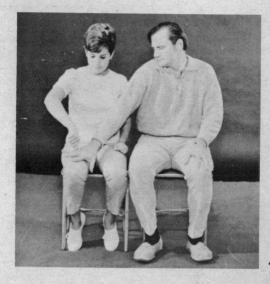

41

41. The situation is similar to the one preceding; he has his hand on your knee; pull it away by gripping the little finger.

42, 43. Your arm is grabbed (this is shown from the rear, it could be from the front); effect release by pulling on his little finger.

44. A rear choke: using a snappy, jerky action, effect release with finger pull.

42

43

44

In the less serious situations the finger pulling action might be enough; in the more serious situations, it would be essential to continue the actions which would complete the defense.

45

VALUE OF THE KICK

The single most important defense for a girl to use is the kick. At least ninety percent of the attacks which might be made involve a reaching or grabbing action. As 45 illustrates, it would be silly for a girl to depend on her fists for self-defense. Not only is her reach shorter than a man's, but punching depends on power and a woman cannot hope to oppose the power of a man's fist with a counter-punch using less power. In order to come within punching distance of a man's face, you would have to place yourself in the most vulnerable position possible.

46

The most sensible action is shown in **46**. Note that a small, slight girl can kick into the knee of a much larger, stronger man *without placing herself within his fist range.*

Most men can block or stop punching blows, but they are not experienced in blocking a kick into the knee or shin. Your leg is stronger than your arm and even without shoes on you can kick with great force.

A relatively small amount of practice will develop your kicking ability surprisingly well.

KICK INTO KNEE OR SHIN

Kicking into the leg, at the knee or shin, is the most effective, practical defense action which can be used by girls. You can kick into the leg from out of fist range or when you are close in; you can kick into the leg of an adversary in front, to the side, or in back of you; you can kick from the ground.

The target area to be kicked at is more important than the style of kick you use. The type of kick used will be partly determined by distance from the adversary and by relative positions.

Whenever possible, do not come within fist range of your adversary to apply a kick. Kicking in close should be done only when you are trapped in close already and cannot get out of range of his hands.

The shin is peculiarly sensitive to pain on most people. Because the shin bone is not protected by muscle or flesh, a moderate kick into the shin causes pain; a forceful kick causes great pain.

Kicking into the knee with force can incapacitate a man or cause sufficient pain to subdue him, or put him on the ground.

The idea of ongoing, continuing defense is essential for serious situations. Repeating the same kick over and over could constitute an ongoing, continuous defense. In mental practice, avoid thinking of delivering a single kick; deliver a series of kicks without hesitation.

HOW TO KICK INTO KNEE OR SHIN

47.   From the front, turn your foot so that the edge is directed toward the opponent. Snap out sharply, hitting with the side of the foot or shoe. This method of kicking is effective from close in and can be done with either foot.

From a very close in body grab, a variation which can be used is to hit with the *inside* edge of the foot or shoe. The rule is to kick in the manner which seems most comfortable.

48.   As you move farther away from your adversary, the bottom of the foot or shoe is a more comfortable style of kicking

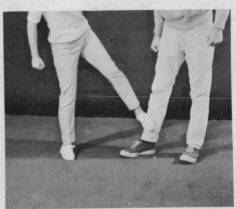

47

48

blow. Since you want to get as far as you can away from your opponent, in mental practice think of stepping or leaping away whenever possible and kicking with the bottom of the shoe.

49.   If your adversary is behind you, turn to look at your target area and kick back into the shin or knee. You can use the bottom or side of the foot or shoe to kick.

50.   If you are behind your adversary (which is a good place to be!), kicking into the back of his knee can cause his leg to buckle. A forceful kick in this manner can put him badly off balance or on the ground.

49

50

51

51. The ball of the foot (or toe) can be used for kicking forward into the shin. More precision is required to make this an effective blow.

TARGETS FOR FOOT BLOWS

The practical striking areas are those shown — into the knee, at the shin, onto the instep and into the back of the knee.

These targets are simple to reach with a kick which can be done by a girl who has basic skill. Striking areas which can only be reached with higher kicks are not practical; they require greater skill and continuing practice to maintain that skill.

CORRECTING MISTAKES OF KICKING TECHNIQUE

Because kicking is the single most important self-defense action you will learn, you should be careful about correcting mistakes as you are learning to kick. Girls learn the kicking techniques very well, but usually make common errors in beginning practice which are serious enough to invalidate the major advantages of kicks for self-defense. Although you are not trying to become an expert in self-defense, you should realize that the correction of these errors is more than technical — it is tactical!

52   Correct this error.   53   Correct this error.

52.   The primary advantage of defending from out of fist range will be lost if you move in too close to your adversary to deliver the kick. You may not always have the choice of defending from out of fist range, but you should always try to keep as far away from your adversary as possible. Compare photo 52 with photo 46; note the relatively vulnerable position into which she has placed herself in photo 52. In practice, avoid moving in close to deliver a kick which can be done from out of fist range.

53.   A stiff-legged kick is not efficient.

To correct the error of kicking stiff-legged, practice the edge-of-the-shoe and the bottom-of-the-shoe kicks as though they were two-part actions.

54   55

54. The first part of the action is bending your leg, exaggerating the degree to which your knee is drawn up.

55. The second part of the action is a snappy, thrusting kick. When you practice this two-part action, position your foot for the correct kick before you thrust out.

Photo 55 shows the correct position for delivery of the edge-of-the-shoe kick. For the bottom-of-the-shoe kick, you would draw your knee up higher and position your foot to strike with the bottom of the shoe before thrusting out.

EXAMPLES OF USE OF KICK

56. Adversary grabs shoulders. You kick into the knee with the edge of the shoe and scrape down onto his shin.

56

57

58

57. With both wrists grabbed, kick into the knee.

58. With both wrists grabbed from the rear, turn to look;
kick into the knee.

59

59. Choked from the rear, begin the defense with a kick back into the knee.

In mental practice, avoid delivering a single kick; think of the kicks in series, continuing as necessary.

STAMP DOWN ON INSTEP

The instep is a vulnerable area, easy to hit and sensitive even when struck through the shoe. Stamp down with the heel of your shoe or with the bottom of your foot. You can use this kick to the front as in 60 and to the rear, as shown in 61.

60   61

EXAMPLES OF USE OF STAMP ON INSTEP

62.   As the man grabs, stamp down on the instep.

63.   From a seated position, stamp onto the instep.

64.   If the person is someone you do not want to hurt, place your foot on his instep and stand on it without stamping. You can do this in a good-humored way and get the desired result.

62

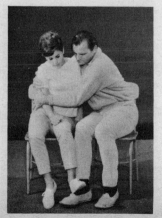

63

64

EXERCISES TO DEVELOP KICKING PROFICIENCY

The defenses you will learn in this course are so simple that you should remember them and be able to use them long after the completion of the instruction.

Moreover, the techniques will work for you whether or not you keep fit. The traditional approach to self-defense assumes that the student will always be in top physical condition. The traditional techniques depend upon the maintenance of a very high level of technical perfection and body conditioning. The sad fact is that a high proportion of young women will not engage in activity to maintain peak physical condition following the school years. So, the defenses have been designed for efficiency regardless of your physical condition.

However, if you are interested in maximum self-defense efficiency, as well as exercises which will help keep you fit, the practice of kicking techniques will be very useful. Kicking is the most important self-defense action you will learn. Kicking practice is the most important way of maintaining self-defense skill.

65, 66.   Grasp your knee and pull your leg in close to your body; thrust outward with vigor. This is not a kick for height, but for thrust. Alternate kicking leg. Maintain your balance. When you can, draw your knee up close to your body without the help of your hands.

65   66

67, 68.   Raise your knee, bend your leg as shown; kick out to the side with a vigorous thrust. Alternate kicking leg. Maintain your balance.

69, 70.   Rising onto the ball of one foot, raise the knee of the other one and kick high. With practice, you should be able to kick as high as your head. Maintain your balance. Although you will never, in practical defense situations, be expected to deliver high kicks, the ability to kick high will greatly improve your practical, low kicks.

67   68

69   70

BALANCE EXERCISE

71-74. Start from relaxed, standing position. Raise one knee and stretch that leg forward; return to the bent leg position and extend the leg behind you, keeping your back straight. The raised leg should not touch the floor in the sequence shown. Alternate this practice, using right and left leg. The movement is slow and gentle, with a flowing action.

Improving your balance enhances your kicking skill and enhances your style of body movement.

71

72

73

74

LEAPING

75, 76, 77.   Leaping is an excellent method of evading a forward, rushing attack. Leaping disconcerts the adversary and it
gets you out of his fist range. When space permits — leap. It is
best to leap to the side; from this position you can deliver a
series of kicks but he would find it awkward to attack. If you
cannot leap out to the side, leap straight back out of fist range
before you begin kicking.

Avoid leaping flat-footed. Leap as lightly as possible, from the
balls of your feet. Loss of balance is common for beginners, but
quite easily corrected with minimum practice. Leaping practice
will enhance graceful body movement as it improves your self-
defense skill.

75

76

77

SLIDE-STEPPING

To improve your style of body movement, here is an exercise which is similar to the fencer's manner or changing position.

The main purpose of this style of movement is to change position without getting into one-point balance. By moving on the balls of the feet, and sliding one foot toward the other, at no time is the balance as weak as when one foot is completely off the floor (as in taking ordinary walking steps). This improved manner of changing position enhances your self-defense training by letting you step from one position to another while maintaining good, strong balance.

78, 79, 80. Start from a T-position. Shift your weight to the ball of the rear foot, with light weight on the ball of the forward foot. Slide the forward foot a normal step to the front. Slide the rear foot up to about six inches behind the forward foot. At no time has either foot been taken completely off the floor. Avoid having the feet placed too close together.

Practice slide-stepping from side to side and from front to rear. Start from the T-position with right foot forward; alternate with left foot forward.

78

79

80

81

82

LEAPING EXERCISE

81, 82, 83. Keeping your body upright, practice leaping from one position to another, without loss of balance. This is not a stepping action, but resembles a dancer's movement. Push off from the ball of one foot and land on the ball of the other, each time. Avoid "clunking" down onto the heel. Try to increase the distance you can leap as you improve balancing skill.

83

With a minimum of practice, you can improve your body-movement style greatly. When you improve your ability to leap, using graceful, pleasing movements, you will improve your style of walking as well.

Leap from side to side, forward and back.

Because leaping is such a good way of avoiding a number of types of attacks, this practice will enhance your self-defense ability.

DEFLECTING AND BLOCKING BLOWS

84.   Not as effective as leaping, but necessary to learn for those situations in which leaping is not possible, is the technique of parrying or deflecting a forward moving attacking arm.
Deflecting or parrying the blow is possible for a girl because it is not strength which makes the technique effective, but quickness of movement. You are not attempting to counter the power of his striking arm, but move it in another direction. If you cannot step to the side, duck or dodge out of range of his arm and deflect the blow. As the attack is made, step to the outside of the striking arm and hit at it with both hands slashing, or with both forearms.

85.   The third choice for stopping or evading an intended blow is the blocking technique. Because it does not take you out of range and because it requires some power, blocking is not as useful as leaping or parrying, but it is sometimes the only technique which is practical.

At the first sign of his attack, block *both* his arms with your forearms or open-handed slashing blows. You block *both* his arms whether or not he attacks with both; this prevents a second attacking blow.

This technique may be used not only against an intended fist attack, but *any* type of forward reaching aggressive action.

Avoid the error of trying to push at a stronger person's arms; without superior strength, this would be ineffective. The correct deflecting and blocking actions are snappy and vigorous.

84   85

ARM BAR: Basic Technique and Two Variations

These are the most simple and useful of the holds. They may be omitted from the shorter courses. When practiced, safety rules must be observed carefully. Partners offer no resistance in practice. Avoid smashing or jerking actions.

86. As partner reaches out, simulate a slash down into the elbow or onto forearm, using your left hand.

87. Right hand grips the reaching wrist.

88. Rotate captured arm to turn back of elbow up; with left forearm simulate striking down onto elbow. Apply pressure by pulling up on captured wrist and pressing down onto the back of captured elbow.

It must be your forearm, not your hand, which is placed at the captured elbow. Don't forget to pull up on the captured wrist.

86

87

88

89

90

91

92

Variation A

89, 90, 91. If, after the wrist is captured, the held arm is pulled up and back, use the force of the resistance to shove the arm back and up, as shown.

92. Pressure is applied by pushing upward on the captured wrist and gripping the collar with your left hand; adversary can be controlled and walked.

Don't forget to grip the collar to assist your action. The captured arm is pulled up, not pushed against, the back.

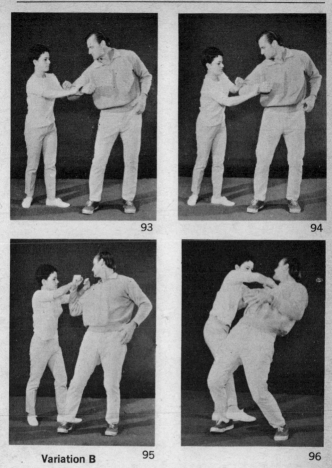

93

94

Variation B 95

96

93-96. If the resistance of the captured arm is forward, use the force of the resistance to move the arm in a circular direction forward, up and toward the shoulder. Your left hand reaches through to grip your own right wrist. If this action is quick and accompanied by a step which places your leg behind the adversary, a kick back throw can be effected while maintaining the hold.

Remember to use body motion to assist in the application of pressure.

WRIST HOLD WITH TAKEDOWN

97. As partner reaches out, slash down into the elbow with (simulated) force to bend the arm.

98. Grip the reaching hand with both your thumbs on the outside of the back of the captured hand as you take a deep step forward.

97

98

99

99. Turning the captured hand counter-clockwise take another step in to place your right leg behind partner's right leg. A continuous turning action assisted by the twist of your upper body effects the takedown.

Your body action should assist in applying pressure. Remember to grip the entire hand, not just the fingers.

THROWS

Traditional judo throws are not suitable for self-defense. They are particularly not suitable for girls' self-defense. Refer once more to photo 45 and you will see the validity of this statement. All throws must be executed from very close in to an adversary. With the exception of *rare* instances, girls cannot reach in to grab for the throwing action without getting into fist hitting range. If you are out of fist range, it is silly to move in close when you can use the kick, which allows you to stay out of range.

The amount of instruction and practice which would allow you to become as proficient at throwing techniques as to make them practical for self-defense is out of the question for most girls. It is out of the question for a school course. The other objection we have to emphasis on throwing techniques is that there is far greater possibility of injury in the practice of throws than in the practice of other, more efficient methods of self-defense. There is no need for you to get hurt in the process of learning not to get hurt!

Observe safety rules scrupulously. Your partner need not be thrown to the ground to let you learn how these techniques work. When you have practiced the correct procedure to the point of breaking balance, you may stop. It will be quite obvious that the ending of the technique would be effective if carried through.

KICK BACK THROW

100.   In order to be used effectively for self-defense, throws must be preceded by kicking and hand blows which weaken the adversary, making him vulnerable to the throwing action.

101.   When adversary has been hurt, grip his shoulders (or sleeves) and twist him around counter-clockwise into awkward balance, as you take a deep step with your left foot. The twisting action is continuous and when balance is broken, kick calf-to-calf with your right leg against his right leg. The leg action is a vigorous, swinging action (not a push) with follow-through so that your kicking leg is brought up high behind you. In class practice, you may execute the calf-to-calf kick with some vigor, but maintain the shoulder grip on your partner to avoid a full throw.

Kick back throw is fun to learn, but not essential for effective, basic self-defense. If time and situation permit, you will enjoy learning to perform the throw correctly. Don't worry about it if you don't!

Avoid twisting your leg around your partner's leg; the proper action is a swinging, thrusting calf-to-calf kick. As you kick, you must use the twisting action of your arms to weaken your partner's balance.

Do not practice this throw beyond the point of breaking balance unless you are supervised by a trained instructor. Do not practice this throw unless you have a mat to work on.

100   101

BACK TAKEDOWN

102.   Following the pre-throwing action to hurt your adversary, get around behind him, to one side, grip at his collar and sleeve and jerk back with vigor as you kick into the back of his knee. Avoid getting directly behind your adversary as this would place you in the path of his fall.

Avoid the tendency to push into the back of the knee; the correct technique is a stamping, vigorous kick. Remember to stand to the side of your opponent, otherwise, you will be in the line of fall.

102

WHEN TO GO INTO ACTION FIRST

No matter how well-trained you are in self-defense, the most sensible behavior is to avoid physical actions. There are instances, however, in which you can make the first move without jeopardizing your chance of talking your way out of the situation.

103.   When you are being threatened, but feel there is some chance of avoiding physical action, assume a well-balanced position of readiness with your arms folded, as shown. From this position, kicks and hand blows may be quickly and easily used, but your posture does not show belligerence or willingness to fight.

104.   At the slightest sign of aggressive action, kick into the shin as you thrust your hand toward his face and YELL! This combination of actions will disconcert your opponent, especially if he does not expect any action at all. Be prepared to continue hitting and kicking as necessary.

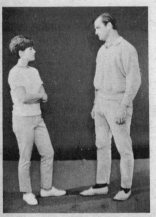 

103   104

RESPONSE TO THREAT OF BACK ATTACK

There is no need to become nervously fearful of attack at **all** times in order to be adequately prepared for defense. There **are** situations in which threat of attack is extremely unlikely **and** there are others in which the threat of attack is possible. Any girl who is not hysterical or pathologically worried about danger can tell the difference. Alone, at night, on the street, there is obviously a different degree of possible danger than there is at a sorority luncheon.

The purpose of the following procedure is to make you able to respond quickly to the slightest sign of possible danger from behind.

You will practice response to three kinds of clues: sound, touch and sight. Sound clues which might indicate danger could be shuffling noises, breathing, or rustling of clothes. A sight clue might be a shadow or it might be something you see out of the corner of your eye — before it comes into the direct line of vision. Response to touch means a response to the slightest touch — before a grab or choke could be fully applied.

105. Partners stand facing the same direction. Partner at the rear will give signals to which the front partner will respond. Some examples of the signals are: A light touch on the shoulder, moving a hand into peripheral vision area, shuffling or other sounds (if conditions permit).

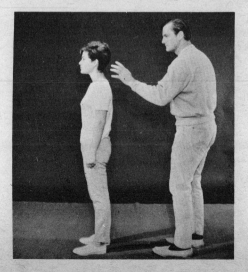

The rear partner should not make the signals too óbvious. The purpose of the procedure is to give some experience in responding to the threat of attack without waiting for the attack to be completed.

106.   At the slightest indication of possible danger, *turn to see what is behind you,* as you prepare to slash and kick with simultaneous blows.

This practice should be done over and over in the session, with the surprise attack coming from either side, alternating touch signal and sight signal. In a room full of girls practicing, it is very difficult to simulate the sound cue. In mental practice, you should prepare yourself for response to sound cues.

Remember to look around to see what you are hitting. Striking out wildly is not as efficient as looking at your target.

106

RELEASES FROM WRIST GRIPS

Both of these release techniques depend on the use of kicking first. A slight girl trying to effect release from the grip of a strong man can use these releases effectively *only* if the kick has hurt and distracted him.

RELEASE FROM ONE WRIST BEING GRIPPED

107.   Adversary has gripped one wrist with both his hands. Kick vigorously into his knee or shin as you grip your own captured hand with your free hand. Make a fist of the captured hand and grip the full fist, for strongest action.

108.   Jerk your arms up cross-body, releasing your captured hand at the point between his thumbs and forefingers, which is the weakest part of his grip.

107   108

109

109. When freed, use kicks and hand blows as required to hurt or subdue your adversary. The same defense will work if he has grabbed with only one hand.

RELEASE FROM BOTH WRISTS BEING GRABBED

110. Both your wrists are gripped, as shown. You kick with vigor until you feel that his grip is somewhat looser.

111. With a quick, jerky action swing both your arms out to the side. Even if your movement is only a few inches out, it can get the desired result.

110   111

112, 113. His natural reaction to your action will be to force inward, opposing your outward movement. When you feel the inward pressure, quickly reverse your arm action to jerk your arms in and up, effecting release at the weakest point in his grip, between thumbs and forefingers. Repeat, if necessary.

114. When free, continue with hand and foot blows, if necessary.

Remember that you cannot pull your arms straight back to effect release from a strong person's grip. You must effect release from the weakest part of the grip — up from between the thumb and fingers.

112

113

114

115   116

RELEASE FROM FRONT CHOKE

115, 116. From a front choke, as shown, it might be awkward for a short, slight girl to hit down onto the adversary's forearms (a defense which we teach to boys and men). Clasp your hands together (do not intertwine your fingers), and thrust your arms upward in a vigorous movement. It is the quickness of the action which insures its effectiveness; both your arms coming up between his elbows in this vigorous fashion can exert enough pressure to make him release his grip or weaken it considerably. In mental practice, you would repeat the action, aiding your defense with a smart kick into the shin, if necessary.

After effecting release, continue with kicking and hand blows, if necessary.

You need not wait to be choked to apply this defense. It works even better if you start the action while he is in the process of reaching; it works against any reaching-out defense and does not have to be reserved for the specific situation of an applied choke.

Note that your elbows should not be held too close together. Aim your upthrusting arms between his elbows, not at the forearms. A push will not be effective; it must be a vigorous, quick action.

DEFENSE AGAINST HAIR PULLING

117.   Your hair is pulled from the front.

118.   Clasp both your hands down onto his gripping hand to relieve the pain.

119.   Maintaining the pressure on his hand, twist your body to hurt his wrist as you kick into his shin or knee as required for release.

Continue the defense, as necessary, with kicks and hand blows.

120.   Your hair is pulled from the rear, as shown. Clasp both your hands down onto his gripping hand and press down to relieve the pain.

117

118

119

120

121

122

123

121, 122. Keeping his hand firmly pressed down onto your head, duck down and twist around to face him. The resulting pain on his wrist could effect release at this point.

123. If necessary, continue your defense, kicking into the shin or knee, as necessary.

COMBINATION OF ACTIONS FOR COMPLETE DEFENSES

In order to get the most out of this course, you should avoid thinking of specific defenses against specific attacks. Think of the actions as a basic "vocabulary" of techniques which you will use in combination. It is this combination of the techniques which makes them complete defenses.

Following are some examples of the combinations of actions. These are not to be learned as rigid responses, but are to be thought of as illustrations of the flexible use of this basic "vocabulary" of defense actions to make a usable "language" of self-defense.

HOW TO PRACTICE COMPLETE DEFENSES

When practicing the complete defenses and when improvising your own examples of complete defenses, you will make better progress if you emphasize continuity of actions, rather than speed.

The continuing, ongoing defense should be done smoothly, without hesitations. When you have become accustomed to the idea of defense as ongoing actions, it will be relatively easy to speed them up.

As a beginner, you will know only a few simple defense actions. An ongoing defense is simply the repetition of those few actions. More sophisticated response is possible when you learn a few more techniques and can use them in varying combinations.

COMPLETE DEFENSE AGAINST FINGER CHOKE

In this example the finger pulling action is the critical first action because you must relieve the choking pressure immediately.

124.   To effect release from the choke, pull with vigorous, jerky action.

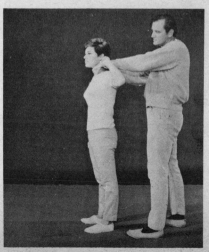

124

125. When the choke has been broken, maintain your hold on one of the fingers as you turn about to face your adversary. Kick into the knee or shin until he is hurt.

125

COMPLETE DEFENSE AGAINST BACK FOREARM CHOKE

126. When a choke is taken from the rear using the forearm, as shown, it would be awkward to try to effect release by pulling on the finger. The pressure of the forearm against the throat is very strong in this type of choke and that pressure must be relieved by turning your head into the bend of his elbow and by gripping his arm with both your hands and jerking down. This dual action is not likely to break the choke, but it will give relief and permit you to continue with the next action, which is to kick with vigor into his knee or shin. Kick until you feel the grip loosen.

127. Only when the grip has been loosened, may you turn your head out of the crook of the elbow. Forceful kicks will cause him to react by moving his body back.

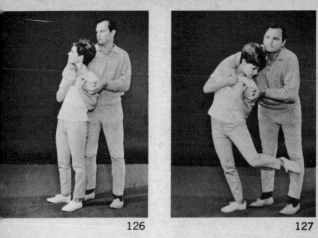

126

127

128

129

128. Take advantage of this movement to step back under his arm and free yourself with a ducking down movement.

129. Maintain your hold on his arm and jerk it upward behind him as you kick with force into the back of his knee.

Continue kicking until he is subdued or hurt.

The movie version of a defense against this attack usually shows the girl throwing the attacker over her shoulder. In the movies this works because the villain is paid to jump over. In real life it does *not* work because it is extremely difficult to throw from this position. Even a girl with years of practice (which would theoretically take her into mature womanhood), might find it impossible to apply a throw from a pulled back off-balance position. If she were to drop down into better throwing position, it would only intensify the choking pain.

No, don't try for the movie solution unless your ambition is to become a stunt girl. In that case, your stunt man partner would take the risk out of using flamboyant, spectacular, and impractical techniques.

COMPLETE DEFENSE USING DEFLECTING ACTION

130.   Deflect the oncoming blow.

131.   Make simultaneous hand blows, one against his forearm and the other into the neck; kick, if necessary.

130   131

132.   Effect a back takedown.

132

LEAPING ACTION AND COMPLETE DEFENSE

The purpose of this practice is the same as that for any of the continuing, combining series: to give you the feeling of carrying through with your defense until you are free to run away or have subdued your assailant.

133.   Leap to the side as the attempted attack is begun.

133

134, 135.   From the side, deliver kicks into the leg, alternating
kicking leg, moving around to the rear of your adversary as you
kick.

134

135

136

136. When you are behind him, direct your kicks into the back of the knee to buckle him down.

When he is visibly weakened, you can effect a back takedown, if necessary.

COMPLETE DEFENSE USING KICKS, BLOCKING BLOWS, AND TAKEDOWN

You will achieve maximum self-defense skill if you can use the defense actions in a flexible manner. The long series which follows, 130-137, is an example of a complete defense which could be useful against many types of attacks. Practice this series as a model. Then, make your own combinations of defense techniques. Develop your ability to use the blocks, leaps, hand and foot blows and takedowns without having to memorize them as rigid routines.

137, 138. Assuming that you are out of fist range of your adversary, kick, turn and kick as your first actions. Deliver the kicks without coming within fist range!

137

138

139.   Block both reaching arms; kick into the shin, 140.

139

140

141.   Deliver a hand blow, high.

142.   Kick again, to the shin. (In mental practice, repeat the kicks and hand blows until the adversary is visibly weakened.)

141

142

143. When adversary is weakened, turn him around with a vigorous thrust at his shoulders.

144. Continue kicking and hitting from the rear, or effect a back takedown.

143

144

DEFENSE FROM THE GROUND: PRONE AND SUPINE

Kicking is the only effective defense in the situations shown.

145.   If you are lying prone (face down), having been pushed or fallen, turn onto your side and deliver kicks in the shin with vigor.

Do not stop kicking until your adversary is hurt or goes away. If you try to rise while he still hovers over you, you are placing yourself in a more vulnerable position than before.

146.   From a supine (face up) position, place your weight onto your forearms, as shown, and kick with vigor into the shin and knee.

147.   To avoid letting him get around to your head, pivot on your forearms and buttocks, keeping your head away from him and continue kicking as you turn.

148.   Continue your turning action and kicking as necessary. Do not try to get up while he is still threatening; wait until you have hurt him or he goes away.

145

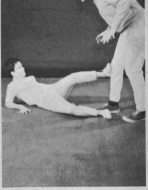

146

147

148

DEFENSE FROM SUPINE POSITION (As from bed)

The possibility of being attacked in bed is slight.

Girls have been made fearful of this type of attack through lurid magazine stories and grisly TV and movie scenes. In real life it happens infrequently.

Irrational fears are just as tormenting as other fears (more so, perhaps) and therefore we are teaching a defense against attack in bed, even though it is unlikely that you would ever encounter this situation, 149.

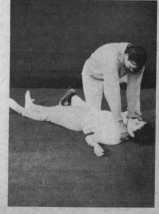

149

150. Slash down on both forearms and continue the defense, hitting into the nose, and poking into the eyes. Continue with hand and finger blows into his face, eyes, and neck, as necessary, 151.

152, 153. Or you can break the choke with the clasped-hand method and then continue with hand and finger blows, as necessary.

150

151

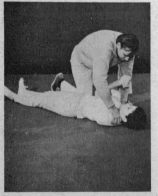

152

153

FORCED ENTRY

If proper precautions are taken, the danger of forced entry can be minimized.

There are, statistically, few entries in which force is used. The common method of gaining entry is trickery, rather than force; the intruder poses as friend, messenger or repairman. Or, he takes advantage of carelessness — an unlocked door, an open window.

In reporting bizarre, sensational crimes, newspapers emphasize the actions of the criminal.

Seldom do we read of the act of carelessness on the part of the victims which might have allowed the criminal to enter without opposition. The victim, being the victim, is shielded from any hint of responsibility. You should realize that the victim often unwittingly helps the criminal. Reread the section RULES OF SAFETY AT HOME. Learn to recognize and avoid the acts of carelessness which permit an intruder to enter.

154.   You are tricked into opening the door, or have left it open, but the adversary has not actually entered.

155, 156.   Hand blows to the face, using finger stabs to the eyes, or heel-of-palm up under the chin could drive him back far enough for you to slam the door.

154   155

157.   Continue with kicks into the shin.

Continue kicking and hitting until he is driven away. SCREAM!

156   157

GUN ATTACK

We are not teaching defenses against guns in this book because such defenses are not easy to learn.

Unexpected, unprovoked gun attacks are statistically rare. Remember that it is the uncommon attack which is reported in the news; the commonplace occurrence is not newsworthy.

Girls who are the victims of gun attacks are usually shot by other family members or by a discarded or jealous boyfriend. If you are involved with a gun-owning man of unstable temperament, you are flirting with violent death.

If you have any reason to fear gun attack, you should get advice and help from the police; this is the only safe procedure.

WHEN TO DEFEND AGAINST AN ARMED ADVERSARY — Knife, chain, etc.

There are some instances in which you can adequately defend yourself against an attack with a weapon. You must prepare yourself *mentally* in advance of such an occurrence or you will not act properly. Many emergencies can be calmly handled if one has had previous advice on what to do. But if you are suddenly confronted with danger and have not the vaguest idea of what you can do to protect yourself, your reaction would probably be panic. In a state of panic you are lost! Do not confuse fear with panic; you can be very frightened and still act prudently if you know what it is you are to do; panic is complete loss of reason.

There are two ways in which a weapon is used: one is for the purpose of scaring you so that you will not resist robbery or burglary; the second is more sinister — that is when the man intends to use his weapon to hurt or kill and that is his only purpose.

If you are threatened with a weapon by a robber or burglar, your only prudent action is to be quiet and let him have your money. You would be very foolish to try and stop him. You can even insure your physical safety by assuring him that you do not intend to scream and that you are less interested in your money than in your life.

You are in less danger of physical harm from a professional thief than from an amateur, but you need not distinguish between them in order to guide your behavior. A primary rule of self-protection is: Don't resist armed robbery!

The man who tries to use a weapon for the *single purpose* of hurting a woman must be handled in an entirely different manner than the thief. The man who wants to do harm for the perverse pleasure of doing harm cannot be reached by reason; he is not open to argument. He cannot be appealed to by begging for mercy; his peculiar pleasure is increased by the helplessness of his victim. In the case of such a threat of attack, you have absolutely no alternative except to make a strong and spirited defense. As always, the advice to use physical defenses is based on the premise that you are unable to resort to flight or that no means of getting help is available to you.

Remember that it is statistically rare, and therefore a subject for news headlines, to be confronted by an unprovoked, unknown assailant. Your preparation to deal with such a rare event is simply a means of increasing your chances of behaving prudently should the unlikely situation occur.

KNIFE ATTACK

If a knife is held on you as a threat, and the motive of the man holding the knife is robbery, give up your valuables. If the attacker really means to use his knife to cut or kill you, you must act! The defenses shown here can be used even if you have only moderate skill; it is your attitude and your determination which make the difference. There is some possibility of being cut on the leg, but it is not as dangerous as being cut in the face or body.

If the attack is made very close in, and you have time, the use of a distracting action is an important aid to your defense. Screaming should accompany your actions.

DEFENSE AGAINST LUNGING KNIFE ATTACK

158.   As the attack is made, leap to the outside of the knife hand.

159.   Without hesitation kick with force into his knee.

160.   Turn and kick again and repeat until he is visibly weakened or hurt. As you deliver the kicks, keep your upper body well back out of range of his weapon.

158

159

160

After you have hurt him, grip his arm (not the knife), with both your arms held out stiffly; continue kicking, as needed until he is subdued.

DEFENSE AGAINST CLOSE-IN KNIFE ATTACK

161. When there is no space in which to leap away, as the knife hand moves forward, side-step to the outside of the knife hand and block with a backhanded motion at his arm.

162. Stab into the eyes. This is one of the situations in which such a defense is warranted and necessary.

163. After hurting him, lock his knife arm out and deliver continuous forceful kicks into his knee as required to subdue him.

161

162

163

DEFENSE AGAINST OTHER WEAPONS:
Chains, Tire Irons, etc.

Regardless of the weapon being used, make a defense only if the alternative is submission to a beating. The defensive actions which can be used for miscellaneous weapons are similar to those for the knife attack. Leap out of range of the weapon hand; rely on kicking as your best defense.

WHEN MORE THAN ONE ADVERSARY ATTACKS

If you are confronted by more than one adversary, your only chance of survival is to apply the defense actions with all the apparent courage you can muster. Two men who attempt to attack a woman or girl are even more cowardly and perverse than a single attacker. That means that they are even less open to reason and your only alternative is to fly into action with your full strength. Rely on kicking as your principal defense. Avoid coming within their fist range, if you can. If you are already within close range, depend on finger stabbing into the eyes and throat.

Behave as though you mean to win and your chance of success is very good! This type of bully takes pleasure in inflicting pain, but he does not expect to be hurt. It is very possible that the first forceful kick into the knee, or the first finger stab into the throat would be enough to stop the attack. Be mentally prepared to continue kicking and hitting until you are free to run or until they run away.

PURSE WEAPONS

Every girl and woman carries with her an arsenal of weapons. All you need to know is how to use them. The use of purse weapons is possible only when you have some warning that you are in a dangerous situation and can reach into your purse, or if your adversary can be made to think that you are merely reaching for a cigarette or some cosmetic item.

The main use of purse weapons is for jabbing, stabbing and slashing. The weapons can be used in a moderate way, to inflict great pain, or to injure.

SOME USES OF PURSE WEAPONS

164.   Stabbing with comb into neck muscle.

165.   Scraping across face with teeth of comb.

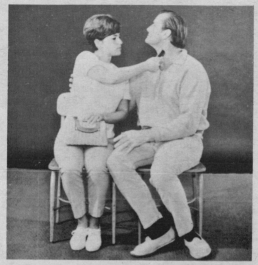

164

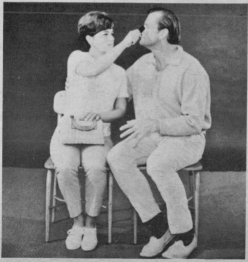

165

166. Jabbing into throat with point end of brush.

167. Stabbing into neck with keys.

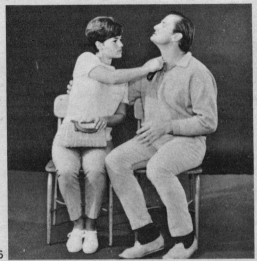

166

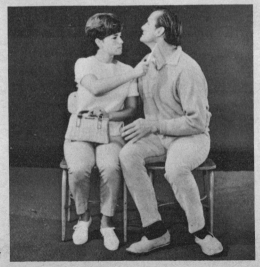

167

168. Stabbing into eyes with keys (in the event of great danger).

169. Jabbing down onto the back of hand with pen or pencil.

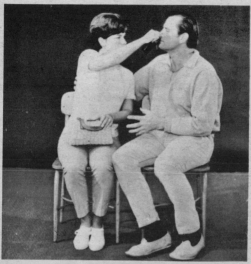

168

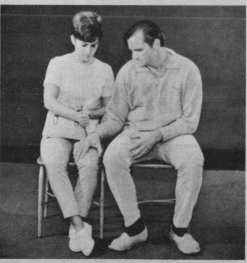

169

Other items which are ordinarily carried in your purse which can be used in similar fashion are: lipstick, mirror, compact, cigarette lighter, etc. For situations which require moderate action, jab into the hand, cheek or neck muscle; for more serious situations, slash across the face or stab into the throat or eyes. In addition to the objects which you carry in your purse, there are many other items which you can use as improvised aids for self-defense, using them in the same manner as suggested for purse items. Examples: ashtray, book, vase.

For really practical self-defense preparation, avoid a dependence on purse weapons. Although they are effective and useful, you ought to be able to defend yourself whether or not purse weapons are available to you. A dependence upon weapons of any kind leads to an increased feeling of inadequacy if the weapon is not available.

CLOSET ARSENAL: Improvising Weapons From Household Items

There are a number of ordinary household articles which can be used as defense aids.

A broom, which is ineffective when used in the usual feminine fashion (hitting down onto the top of the head with the brush area), is a very effective self-defense aid when used properly.

170, 171.   Hold the broom (or mop) with the stick end pointing forward and jam or thrust into the midsection or head.

170   171

Hold the broom (or mop) horizontal and use it for blocking (172), keeping it in position as you begin kicking actions (173), or hit down onto both reaching arms (174) and retaliate with a sharp upward action under the chin (175).

172

173

174

175

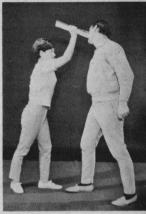

176   177

176, 177. Even a newspaper or magazine, rolled up, can be converted into a self-defense aid if used properly. Avoid slapping actions which are not effective; use the rolled-up paper as a thrusting, jabbing weapon. Continue, as required, with jabbing, stabbing blows with the paper as you deliver a series of kicks until you have hurt or driven away the assailant.

If an intruder is trying to get in and you have time to prepare, you can use household ammonia as a weapon. A glass of ammonia thrown into the face of an assailant will seriously curtail his fighting ability. A glass of ammonia may be used as a threat against an intruder if you seem determined to use it.

DEFENDING AGAINST DOGS

A barking dog is not an attacking dog. If you are afraid of dogs, you have undoubtedly had more experiences of being frightened by them than of being bitten. If you can avoid a dog by taking a detour, do it.

If you cannot avoid coming close to a dog which *appears* to be unfriendly, you could avoid being attacked by your apparent command of the situation.

Dogs respond to command in both senses of the word. Large dogs, particularly, are likely to have been trained to obey certain commands made in a commanding tone. Usually the command words which they are trained to obey are: DOWN, STAY and SIT. But it is not the words alone to which they respond; it is the tone of voice in which they are given. You should use the words familiar to them, and avoid using phrases such as "go away" or "leave me alone" to which they are not accustomed.

Do not shriek; try not to betray your fear. Most dogs, if commanded in the proper manner, will retreat or keep their distance.

In addition to giving the command, if you have time in which to prepare yourself, if there is something like a sweater, coat or similar garment available, wrap it around your forearm and keep that arm out toward the dog. If you do not have anything to wrap around your forearm, you could get your purse ready to hit with.

If you are being rushed by a mad or angry dog, you could take one of two courses of action. You could either start kicking immediately, or you could parry the dog's head or body and then begin kicking. Kicking must be directed into the throat of an attacking dog. This is the most vulnerable area and it is usually presented because of the way dogs raise their heads to attack. Best methods of kicking are with the edge of the shoe or bottom of the foot. Avoid trying to kick with the toe; too much precision is required. *Continue* kicking until the dog runs away.

If a dog has already got hold of you, do not try to pull yourself free; instead, push in the same direction as it is pulling. If you try to pull away, you will assist the tearing action of the dog's teeth. As you push, kick into the dog's throat (if possible) and (if necessary) use finger stabs into its eyes.

If a dog has bitten you and runs away, you *must* make a note of its appearance and the street names where it happened and you *must* immediately report the incident to the police. If you do not do this or if you delay doing it, you may subject yourself to the painful Pasteur treatment. A bite from a rabid dog could mean severe illness or even death.

If the dog which has bitten you can be tested for rabies, or if it can be identified as having been given shots against rabies, you need not undergo the Pasteur treatment.

FLEXIBILITY

Keeping your body flexible, keeps your body youthful. A creaky body is synonymous with "old age." You can begin to practice, right now, to be a beautiful woman and even a beautiful old lady, if you want to.

Maintaining body flexibility is a matter of stretching the connective tissue which holds the body together. In the very young, this connective tissue is springy. In the young, it is very flexible. After the age of 25, unless some sort of stretching activity is given to your body, the connective tissue becomes more and more inflexible until bending and rotating movements become increasingly difficult and awkward.

A minimum program of stretching will keep your body youthful and easy to use. Unless you can easily touch your toes with your fingertips (with your legs straight), you need stretching exercise daily!

178-182.   The simple stretching exercises illustrated, if done for just a few minutes each day, will keep your body flexible and well-functioning.

Inflexibility is a major cause of back pain and back injury; stretching exercises will help you avoid back ailments.

Never force or strain when you are doing stretching exercise. If you are in normal health, you should be able to achieve the flexibility shown in photos, if you engage in a daily routine for only a few minutes every day.

If your body is very inflexible when you start to exercise, you will feel some pain at first. If extreme pain persists after you have been exercising for a few days, you are either forcing too hard, or there is some body malfunction. After easing up, if pain still persists, you should see a doctor. Only a physician is qualified to diagnose an ailment and prescribe a remedy.

178

179

180

181

182

INDEX

BRUCE TEGNER is a specialist in self-defense and sport forms of weaponless fighting whose entire life has been devoted to the field.

He was, literally, born to the teaching of self-defense. Both his parents were professional teachers of the judo-jiu jitsu arts and they began to train him when he was two years old! Until he was eight years old, his mother and father taught him fundamentals. After that, he was instructed by Oriental and European experts.

In a field where most training is limited to a single phase of the work, Mr. Tegner's background is unusual. His education covered many aspects of the various types of weaponless fighting, such as aikido, savate and sword and stick fighting. He holds black belts in karate and judo.

Although he was trained in the old, rigid style of instruction, Mr. Tegner began to introduce innovations as soon as he began to teach. In selection of techniques, as well as in the method of teaching, he developed a system of self-defense more suited to modern use and more appropriate to our culture.

Mr. Tegner taught instructors in the U.S. Armed Forces, and he coached sport judo teams. He has taught men, women and children. He has taught exceptionally gifted children and he has taught disabled and blind students. He has trained actors and invented fight scenes for films. He has devised a special course of instruction which is used by law enforcement agencies and college police science courses. From 1952 to 1967 he had his own school in Hollywood. He now devotes his full time to writing, research and teacher-training. Bruce Tegner has 25 books in print, with additional titles in preparation.

ALICE McGRATH has been teaching and researching self-defense for women and girls since 1957, when she began her instruction at Bruce Tegner's school.

She has taught self-defense in private and class lessons and was the manager of Mr. Tegner's school from 1960 to 1967.

In 1967 and 1968, Miss McGrath taught at the California Physical Education Workshop which is held annually at California Polytechnic State College. The purposes of the workshop are to promote professional advancement and provide in-service education for women teaching in secondary schools.

Miss McGrath and Mr. Tegner have given lecture-demonstrations and have conducted special classes for physical education teachers in high schools and colleges and have appeared together on television and radio programs to talk about and demonstrate their new concept of practical self-defense for girls and women.